Seasons of Time

The Journey of Living

Kelly Ann McMillin

Seasons of Time ~ The Journey of Living

Copyright © 1998 by Kelly Ann McMillin

All rights reserved. All rights to the intellectual property, written word of this collection (in whole or in part), original artwork, and photographs are the sole property of the author. No part of any text or image of this book may be reproduced in any form by any means, electronic or mechanical, without advanced written permission from the author.

ISBN: 978-0-615-45334-7

I would like to give special mention to Obsidian Dawn for the awesome digital brushes and designs that I have incorporated into my own work. I highly recommend you check out the talent at www.obsidiandawn.com from brushes to tutorials.

The Beginning...

I dedicate the seasons of my life and all I shall ever do now and forever to the true loves of my life ... my beautiful daughters, **Samantha** and **Karaline**. You are the warmth of my winter and the joy of my fall. To my littlest angel unseen, I give thee all a mother's love.

Love Always,
Mommy

To Keith,

I could fill a book on just our journey in love and our discoveries of who we really are and what we want out of this life together. We have seen sunrises over the ocean and the dancing starlight upon the waves. We have been battered by storms, separated by the crashing waves of unsettled seas...

But, in the darkest hours our love has been the "true north" that has guided us back to the safe harbors of the other's loving embrace. I know whatever may come on the waves of life that our love will continue to navigate our journey together.

Love Always,
    Kelly Ann

Acknowledgments

First and foremost, I want to recognize my mother, **Mary Ann Salopek McMillin**, who has always pushed me to strive for better, loved me, even when I have not always loved myself, and always a strength I can pull from. Thank you for all of your feedback on my book and since I started showing you poems at 13 years-old that's a lot of feedback.

As a family, I would like to thank my father, **Larry B. McMillin**, and my two brothers, **Bryan** and **Scott**. We have all come a long way down the road of struggles, understanding and growth. I would not be where I am today without you, my family. Dad, I am proud of the man you have worked to be and I know your love has helped keep our family together. Bryan, may you look on life through clearer windows and see the future is what you make of it. Scott, like a falling star not meant to stay, I kept my promise to you and I have not and will not say goodbye. You are with me now as you were then and someday we will ride Haley's Comet.

I would like to take the time to thank the teachers who have entered my life. **Mrs. Knox** I will always think of you fondly, my first teacher and friend. **Mrs. Polk** I will always be grateful for challenging me to be more and not letting me push my education aside. **Mr. Spaulding** for seeing there was more to me then the gothic girl who first walked into your Graphic Arts class. John, you gave me the life raft when I was drowning. **Dr. Jace Condravy** and **Dr. Valerie Swarts** for showing me the kind of strength and compassion women are made of and giving my soul a new awakening.

I have known the gems of love that fill the life span of the heart. Precious are these treasures that color the soul. I thank you for the moments we shared in a world beyond the whispers of the wind, sometimes the climax, sometimes the fall, but forever a part of my story to which I have told with a brush of paint or pen to paper.

I have been blessed to know such friendships that can only come from the heart. The dearest of these friendships is the one I have with you **Jill**. You have been my friend since the 6th grade, my partner in crime, my twin. You were with me the first time I got my first kiss (thanks for rescuing me), first dance outside of school and first hot wings in a thunder storm. Yes, there have been times you needed to pin this bull down to see reason between crushes and reality. But of all of these, I treasure the friendship that has matured over the past few years and that you remain someone that can know and see all of me and still call me friend. I know without doubts that you are there for me, even in the days we do not talk. There is comfort in the strength of our friendship and I am blessed to have a friend who has always helped me see the strength in me.

Jodi, along, with the hours of calls growing up, you gave comfort when Scott died (reminded me that I did not) and that my friend is something I will never forget. Nor our big adventure where you showed me the survival dating skills that brought Keith into my life.

Brandon, who would have guessed that class clowns, could be so serious. So when you see a koala, smile and think of me and the mysteries of the willow tree.

To the "**Old Crew**" and first love, we sure knew how to stir things up. Rides to school (thanks **Beckie**), going to breakfast club, Vo-Tech, Senior Skip Day, 3 hour phone calls, tagging signs, cruising the main strip, slow gin and fires and that only touches the surface of our senior year. Yes, I can say without hesitation that Merriman Drive is a home within my heart and I am glad to have our children share in those joys as we once did. **Jody**, I will never forget my first visit and I am glad not to have seen my last. Thanks to the Gods for giving me a chance to know you, my dearest friends, twice in one lifetime.

Finally, to **Brighid**, you have forged inspiration and passion back into my life. You have given me the final push to bring my book to closure. You have helped me to remove the last filter of my well of life and the water runs freely within me now…

Prelude

I started to capture my emotions at an early age in both writing and drawing. Seasons of Time began to take shape my junior year of high school when I begun placing my poems in seasonal groups based on emotional tone.

My view of life is circular and the reoccurring seasons remind me that what I feel now is already turning to another range of emotions to enrich the experience of living. One should be aware that life is changing, not linger in the past nor stagnate in the present but absorb from it what you can to be used the next time around. The past is just a marker of time and not what defines us ... only the character of how you live in this moment can you drape yourself before the judges. At times, naked one will stand, not for the lack of binding the threads of experience into cloth, but from cutting them away with excuses.

This collection is about the journey of living from innocence to maturity and all it encompasses of both life and death. Though there are elements with a clear influence of Christianity, I make no declaration of what beliefs one should follow. I strongly feel that the connection to the forces and energy all around is a personal discovery and a path like our prints at birth, unique with none the same.

Currently, I am traveling my own path and have come to accept there are a great many things that have become merely the wizard behind the curtain. Yet, when in the presence of life's true mysteries you feel it with all that you are and need not be told it is true. I feel a great comfort in the fact that I have begun the journey into my own heritage both the Celtic and Croatian culture that runs through my heart.

The sections of the book are based on the natural seasons; however, the names are based on my understanding of the Celtic year and festivals. The Celtic people of Ireland viewed the year in two equal halves, Samhain, side of dark, and Bealtaine, side of light. Dividing these halves are the harvest festival of Lughnasadh and the spring festival of Imbolc. The Celtic year begins November 1st, but I have started my collection in the fall harvest festival of Lughnasadh, a time of year where memories abundant dance in my head like the leaves in which my brothers and I played. Later, it would be the season in which Scott's spirit would take flight within the cloak of night. In honor of my brother, the first poem before my collection is one he wrote about courage while we were still in school. It is followed by a poem from each of my daughters.

     I feel a close bond with the triple Goddess Brighid of The Tuatha Dé Danann (known to some as Saint Brigit) who is the patron of poets and bards. She is a triple Goddess who represents the fire of inspiration, the fire of hearth and the fire of smithcraft. I am honored to be a keeper of her flame on the 19th shift and hope that my work may encourage others to create.

Courage

Courage is being brave in the nick of time.
Courage is being a leader for the people in the time of need.
Courage is doing something that is very dangerous.
Courage is overcoming deadly feats to save someone's life.
Courage is meeting a challenge in a game,
And not cheating after someone else cheats and wins.
Courage is helping someone who is not in the coolest
Group, of seventh grade on homework.
Courage is not telling lies when it's easy to get out
Of something by telling lies. Courage is wearing your
Own style of jeans or t-shirts, even when the coolest
Group doesn't like it. Courage is putting yourself
On the line for someone else. Courage is being a good
Friend or brother or sister and helping your family and
Friends stay off of drugs and alcohol.
Courage is... well, you get the picture.

By the Late Scott L. McMillin

-1989-

The Dream Catchers

In the distance way up high, in the velvet night sky, if you look closely it will catch your eye.

It glimmers and shines, glowing with a magic light that catches dreams in the night.

It's filled with a heart's desire, burning with a passionate fire.

This light holds nightmares, sins, everyone's confessions and their darkest secrets untold. If you listen closely their stories will begin to unfold.

Up in that never ending sky, all those stars are souls of the past watching over us. If you look up to their light you may see all their beauty and the history that to others without an open mind, those that evil has made blind, is a mystery.

By Samantha – Age 14

Love

Love is a word that could mean many things,
Like kind, sweet, caring and most of all warmth.

Love can lead to marriage that can lead to fights,
But at the end love is there once more.

So don't forget love is in the air. It can find a way to you.

By Karaline – Age 9

Table of Contents

PRELUDE I

    Courage III

    The Dream Catchers IV

    Love V

LUGHNASADH 1

    October Winds 3

    Not One Tear 6

    Life 7

    The Beat 7

    The Gift 9

    Tell Thee 10

    If I Were 11

    My Unspoken Secret 13

    Fading Friendship 14

    The Little One 15

    Liquid Words 15

    Longing Desire 16

    Could There Be 18

    A Cross of Gold or Stone 19

Time of the Beating Drum	20
A River Rose	22
Life is but a Teardrop	23
Words	24
Some words bring you pain and sorrow.	24
A Letter from the Heart	25

SAMHAIN 27

Hear No Pain	29
World of Ice	31
The Wall	31
A Combat Nurse's Plead	32
Silent is Night	33
A Heart of Many Wounds	34
Just One Touch	36
Kris, My Childhood Friend	37
The Road I Travel	38
Angel not Far	40
My Darling, My Love	41
Only Friends	42
Angels Weep	43
Once	44
Blind Heart	45

Silent Lonely Tears 47

The One Who Gave Me Pain 48

Why the Willow Weeps 49

IMBOLC 51

Love's New Birth 53

Always in My Heart 54

Mother 56

A Mother's Song 57

Sleep Tight 58

Mother's Day 59

First Star 60

Into the Mystic 62

Time is All We Need 64

My Love 65

Friends 65

Sun 66

Birds 66

Brothers 67

Friendship 67

I Say I Love You 68

What I am Thinking Of 70

The Sunshine of My Life 71

Finding My Way to You 72

When It's True 73

Serenity by the Lake 74

When Love Shines on Me 76

The Beginning 77

BEALTAINE 79

Time's Whisper 81

The Road 81

Angel of the Night 82

Sweet Child of Mine 83

Reality's Dream 86

More Than a Thought to Me 88

Love's Prayer 90

Summer's Long Hot Nights 91

I Don't Want to Wait 93

Heat 94

Inside the Heart 95

A Lover's Dream 97

Three Words 98

Tender Nights 99

The Man I Love 100

If you Ask Me... 101

In the Whisper of a Wave 104

About the Author 108

Seasons of Time ~ The Journey of Living

"Our hour here truly unknown,
like breaking clocks with time to go." ~ Kelly Ann

October Winds

I remember, when the autumn winds came,
And took you away.

We talked about our grandma,
We lost in May.

I was seven months with child.
When you saw me, you had smiled.

If only I would have looked, into your eyes.
I would have seen. You were saying good bye.

As I went to sleep,
Before the dawn, I would weep.

While you began an angel's flight,
I would cry, into the night.

God, could not wait,
And not far from home,
You found heaven's gate.

Oh, my sweet brother,
For only a moment, you came to our mother.
But, you could not stay,
For the autumn winds, carried you away.

I heard their knock, as I sat silently, in the dark.
Our parents had to come, and break my heart.

The October winds, I still hear.
As the pain of losing you, I still bare.

**In Loving Memory of Scott L. McMillin
October 19, 1997**

Lughnasadh

"Voice Beyond the Wind" – McMillin '05

Not One Tear

Please my dear ones cry not one tear for me.
Do not be sad; do not be mad.
This I plead, for I now can see the true beauty of life.
Life is something we think will always be.
We plan each day, because we think there will be another.
Until one day, we can see all that can be taken away.
Then we wish we spoke the words never spoken to each other.
Who knew we would never see each other again.
We rush by life not stopping to be glad for what we've got.
Now, I can see the preciousness, which passed me by.
The colors of life which I've ignored.
So I plead, cry not one tear for me.
I know this will be hard. When times seem grim,
But remember me with a grin.
Remember me having fun.
Remember me, and not the pain.
Remember what I have gained.
A place where I'll always feel loved,
No one can hurt me now.
No one can take away the peace I have found.
I walk with my creator through the light, which gives me eternal life.
So not one tear for me,
For I am and always will be in your memories.

Life

From the ground, to the sky above,
Life is pain. Life is love.
Life is to ask the question why,
And know the answer we will find,
In a journey, throughout time.
Life

The Beat

There is a beat, from a drum.
You can't see it.
So from it, you cannot run.
Found, in a dream's farthest depths.
You will feel it, with every breath.
In sleep, it's a rhythm,
A melody so sweet,
A tune, a sort of ancient chime,
Like a mortal clock, keeping time.

The Gift

It is almost your birthday and I have not forgotten.
I think I know what you've been wanting.

But, I would need the help of another,
If I am to get a gift to you, my sweet mother.

It would have to be someone I trust,
So I inspired my sister to pick up a brush.

In every stroke of color she would show,
That life in me still flows.

As she placed her brush down,
Tears fell without a sound.

In that moment she would see,
The gift for you was me.

Tell Thee

Heart not cry.
Eyes not bleed.
Tears of sorrow.
Blood of pain.
Love will come again.
Peace shall be.

Heart not speak.
Eyes not feel.
Words of hatred.
Cuts of revenge.
Good will prevail.
Life begins again.

Heart not judge.
Eyes not convict.
Those of poverty.
Those of shame.
Behold, Heaven's gate of gold will open.
Love and peace, life will unfold.

If I Were

If I were a warm autumn breeze,
I'd blow down all those piles of leaves.
While the children played,
I'd warm up a dreary day.

If I were a tornado,
I'd destroy every other thing in my way.
Men would see that nature rules,
Not their intervention.

If I were, a rainbow,
I'd be red, yellow, blue and green.
I'd rise high, and all the children would see me.
They would wonder if at the end lay a pot of gold.

If I were a thunder storm,
I'd turn the sky to the darkest black.
I'd flash my lighting, and bang my thunder,
Showing all of nature's wonder.

Seasons of Time ~ The Journey of Living

"First Fall" ~ McMillin

My Unspoken Secret

Sometimes life isn't fair, and there are things you just can't bear.
There are things you want and need,
But for the moment they are out of reach.
Have you ever seen a rainbow, or a star that caught your eye?
You can try to reach them, but they are not yours to keep.
You are the rainbow. I want to hold.
You are the star, which shines so bold.
You are the one, I want to kiss.
But, if we did, it would be our friendship I would miss.
There is a fire greater then lust.
A fire, in the heart, of a friend, I could trust.
A love, a love I cannot hold. A love, which cannot be told.
I love you, as a friend.
I love you, as a lover.
I love you more, then any other.
To my heart these words I keep, my rainbow out of reach...

Fading Friendship

There was the good.
There were the bad.
There was the happy and yes, the sad.
Time has made me wonder, about the friendship, we once had.
Our childhood years are fond within my heart,
Even though our friendship was torn apart.
I still want to hold onto the idea it still exists.
But, day by day, I wonder why
I hold on to friendship, which has died?
Like a rainbow in the sky,
Bright and full of life,
But it too fades away.
Not so different from us, in our younger days.
Like the rainbow, we are fading and pulling apart.
Yet, those fond memories will always remain in my heart.

The Little One

Our little one sent from above,
Would fill our hearts with love.

But before we would be united under God's grace,
Our angel would leave this place.

Our little one would have to go,
For reasons we will never know.

But the love that started inside me did not die.
In the Kingdom, he waits for you and I.

Liquid Words

These words make no sound.
From our eyes, they can be found.
Expressed when softly crying,
As if the very soul was dying.
They come from a laughing fool,
Or from the new life we hold.
Between heaven and hell
These words will tell
The story of a man,
For the rest of us
To understand.

Longing Desire

I wanted to tell you, for so long.
My feelings for you are strong.
I tried to hide the love deep inside.
Just waiting, would these emotions die.
But, I just couldn't let them go, and now you know the truth,
About the secrets, which I keep.
The fantasies, of how our bodies will meet,
In the dark, with only a light from within our hearts.

Lughnasadh

"Distant City" – McMillin '05

Could There Be

Could there be love, without hate?
Could there be joy without, sorrow?
Could there be early, without late?
Could there be today, without tomorrow?
Could there be day, without night?
Could there be happy, without sad?
Could there be wrong, without right?
Could there be good, without bad?
Could there be life, without death?

You must experience the bad.
To know when, it is good.

How else would you know you were happy,
Without feeling sad?

How would you know love,
If you never knew hate?
Would you just take it on faith?

A Cross of Gold or Stone

To ask a man now, what cross would
Show the beauty of our lord? He
Would surely pick, a cross of gold.
Yet, that gold does not shine, with the
Brightness of God, but from the greed
Of mankind. I ask, do they wear the
Cross for gold, or for God. If I could
Ask, a man that walked on water, not that long ago. What cross would show the beauty of his
Lord? He would surely pick a cross of stone. The stone would not shine from false brightness, like
A Golden cross, but it would brighten up with your love for God. Remember Jesus drank from a
Carpenter's cup. The stone may be rigged and imperfect. But, it was because mankind was not
Perfect, that Christ the lord lost his life for our souls. Maybe a cross should not be perfect, and it
Should show the flaws of us all.
Do not be fooled, by false beauty.
Behold the true beauty deep inside
Us all. If you believe, and truly
Love God. Then a stone cross will
Shine brighter, then a star of
Gold. A cross of gold or of stone.
Which one would you choose? But,
Choose for God's glory not yours.

Time of the Beating Drum

Long ago, in the fog and mist with a blowing wind,
You could hear the hum, of the beating drum.
thump, thump, thump
A drum of the native's call to the beast. It beats for the lonely.
It beats for the brave, and for every soul, in their grave.
thump, thump, thump
You can hear its rhythm, through the valley of the lost spirits.
It's the life blood of nature. It beats out the thoughts of the creator.
thump, thump, thump
But it is lost, in the dawn of a new age. Where magic and mystery
Have no place. Only some can hear. Hearts of gold they bear.
Few will see it as it beats, forever more like tears of the forgotten Gods.
It beats a path to the promise land. The sound
Is like a hand, to cradle and care, to all that hear.
thump, thump, thump

Lughnasadh

"The Wild" – McMillin '97

A River Rose

There are roses in the river of time.
Petals of those who fill the waters of my mind.
Petals of dreams, these roses in the stream that never wash to shore.
Petals out of reach to the edge of fallen waters they are lured.
A bitter sweet nectar between petals and the thorns.
Though… love is greater than the river's rush my dear friend.
For love is the hand that can pick the petal from the river's bend.

Life is but a Teardrop

A tear moves slow at first, like the beginning
Of a new life. Gradually as time moves on,
So does the tear move faster, and like a rollercoaster,
It picks up more and more speed. As a young mind,
Thirst for more and more information.
The tear begins the decline, like a young body growing old.
Until the tear drops off ones face,
Like an old man whose end is near.
Falling like the hope of man.
Then the time must come. When the tear hits the ground.
The last gasp of a dying man.
The tear evaporates, like the newly released spirit.
Pulled to the sky, by forces it does not control.
Many tears are shed,
Like many lives are lived.
But, for all someday
It ends...

Words

Some words bring you pain and sorrow.
Others make you think of tomorrow.
Why words we only speak?
Why some we only teach?
Words of love, to bring us together.
Words to live by.
Words to die by.
While others make you cry.
Such confusion, it seems we are all loosing.
So many words to choose from,
Yet we only pick the ones for pain.
What could we possible gain?
To know we cause someone to hurt.
To stomp someone's feeling, in the dirt.
Do we even know, we cause such chaos?
Looks like somehow we all lost.
While our souls pay the cost.
Words that bring tears,
Or let go of fears.

Words

A Letter from the Heart

Dear Scotty,

I wanted you to know, I haven't forgotten your birthday. A card would not do, for Heaven gave no address to send one to you.

Many things have happened, many that you missed. At times, I know I feel you, but there are things time will not heal. The clock won't ring your laughter, no face to show your smile, only counting minutes in a day without you now.

So, I am left here not whole. I've done my part to fill it, there is nothing I can do, for God; he knows there is only one of you.

I am told you are happy in the Kingdom I cannot find. But I know better Scotty, Heaven is a place where angels can cry.

There was a promise I made you, the day I had to walk away. The words goodbye, I still refuse to say.

Love Always,
Kelly Ann

Seasons of Time ~ The Journey of Living

"Twilight" – McMillin '93

Samhain

Seasons of Time ~ The Journey of Living

"Only in nature can it be found.
The greatest sound you will ever hear
is the whisper of angels in your ear." ~ Kelly Ann

Hear No Pain

Glass all around the emptiness, of what seems like a bottomless pit.
The air is cool, slowly killing the soul.
Trapped behind the tinted glass, locked away from realities path.
Nothing left, but fear's most painful wraith.
They hear no pain…
Cries of help, no one hears. The forgotten life seems bare.
Fighting through the empty tears when it seems nobody cares.
They hear no pain…
Only fading laughter, in the pouring rain.
You try to break free. Shattered puzzle pieces, of the soul, lying beneath your feet.
Memories of your life repeat.
Will your call be heard at all or will madness bring a fall?
They hear no pain…
Your hands are bleeding, as if your heart is pleading.
Desperate calls, no one answers.
Raising your hands asking the question why.
Life's blood runs out your veins.
They hear no pain…
Too late for you the blood tinted glass.
Now there's no looking back.
Friends will say," You looked happy just the other day."
They hear no pain…
Now you see no pain, and you do no more.

As you rot, in your grave, scattered remains… you feel no pain…

Seasons of Time ~ The Journey of Living

"Trapped" – McMillin '05

World of Ice

The world we hold seems so cold.
Oh, what a tragedy. Greed before love. War before peace.
What kind of future will there be?
The sea of compassion, dried by hate.
We have sealed our own disastrous fate.
From Heaven we've turned.
To Hell we will burn.
Unless our hearts we free, of this evil seed.

The Wall

Step up closely, to hear the whispers, of the time.
Spoken softly, the peoples cry,
Of the living, and those who have died.
Black and glossy. Warm to touch.
Reach out, and hold a name.
Never forget. No one should die in vain.
A name is all we have, of a lover, of a friend,
Of a father, and of a brother.
Nothing else remains. No one to hold.
Just the whispers of the time, on a black wall they are told...

A Combat Nurse's Plead

I sit here, hands stained with blood. My mind stained, with the faces of the dead. While cries and pleads for life, dance in my head. Sometimes, I hear them calling for their families, wives and friends. I find myself telling them things, which never happened. Giving them peace of mind, before their life will end. But, somehow you feel. You've cheated the dead.

Sometimes bullets fly past your head, but all I can see are the dead. I wonder how those who have never fought. Can say it's worth the human cost. Yet, they are not here when the bill needs paid.

I sit here and plead. Why must I be here? Why do the young pay? Where is our God, and why must I see their pain? When only a few, I can save. The smell of death is all around, and no path, of escape, can be found

Yet, still more will die. I see them in my dreams. I hear their screams call me in the dark, and I feel their pain run threw my heart. I pray no more will fight.

I sit here every night, and plead for the end. But, the blood won't leave my hands, and those who have stained my mind won't leave. Another sleepless night will come for me. I wonder, who will explain this all to me? Who will explain it to them? The living wounded and the dead.

I plead, when will it all end...

Silent is Night

Silent is night when angels take flight.
You rest in a land with gates the angels guard.
While pain takes my heart and makes it hard.

Silent is night when the body sheds life.
Time out of reach those things dear.
Hear me angels, set me free.
Help me except what must be.

Silent is night when angels touch the ground.
Where is the peace I once found?

"Lost" – McMillin '05

A Heart of Many Wounds

I bear a heart, of many wounds in this hollow soul I wear.

Wounds from lovers.
Wounds from those who once cared.
Wounds from many others.

Not the smile from my lips, nor the laughter I do sing,
Can hide the tears, which run down my face.
Nor can they fill the place, in my heart,
I bear forever now erased.

Wounds from life.
Wounds from death.
Wounds from a greater emptiness.

I am lost, in the shadows of grace, and one by one all my fears I must face.
No longer does my spirit shine. For a muddy pebble glows of a brighter light.

Wounds from friendship.
Wounds from a larger pain.
Wounds from a loved lost in the fallen rain.

As I walk, just a frame am I, for nothing is possessed on the inside.

Samhain

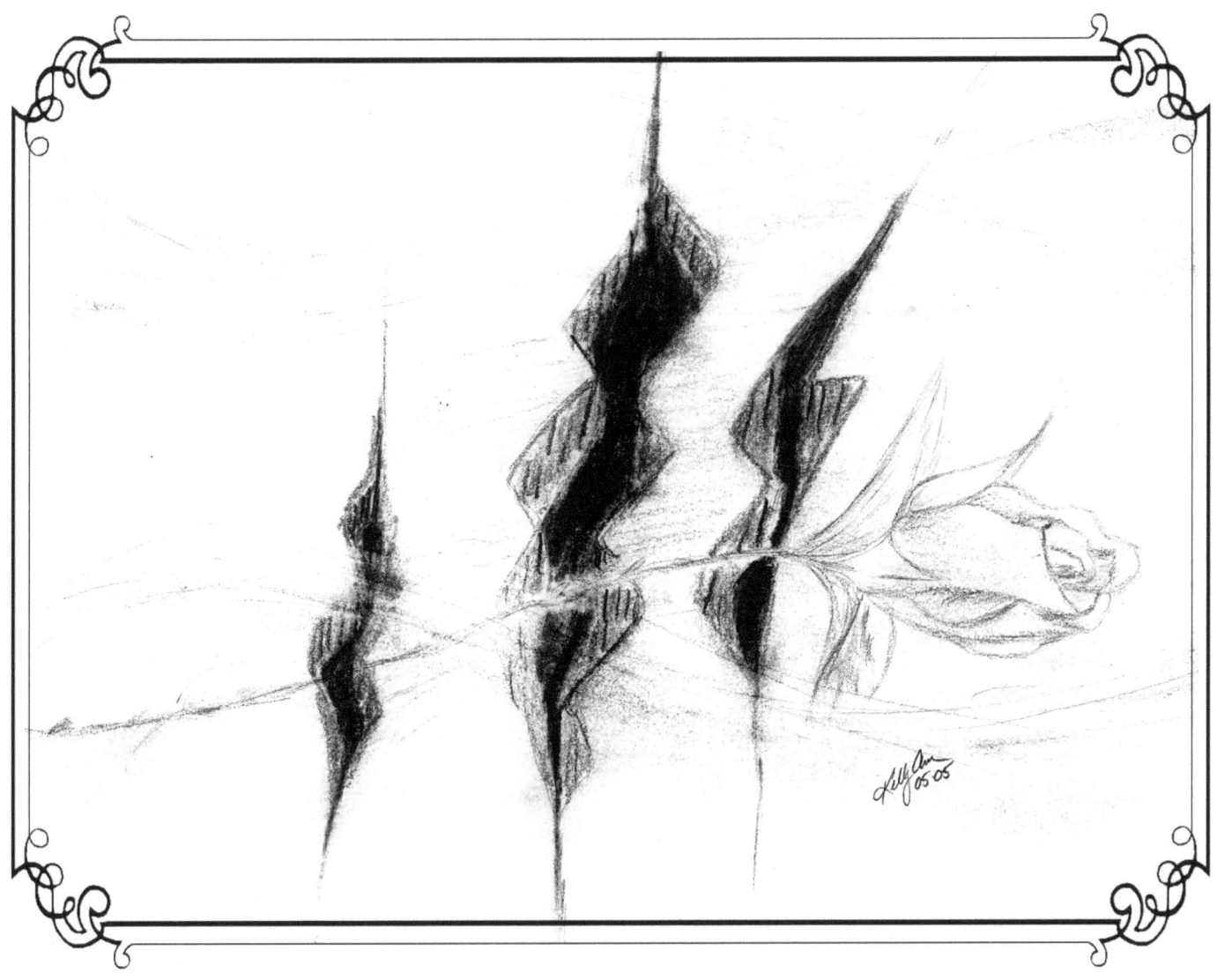

"No Words" – McMillin '05

Just One Touch

I sit, and gaze out my window, upon the darkest night.
I can see us dancing, in the pale moonlight,
As a cool breeze washes over me.

The stars look sad upon me,
And they feel my misery.
They know I long for your arms.
One touch is all I ask. One touch of your lips.
One touch of your hand, yet from all of this I am band.

Here I sit, watching the night.
Angel's wings flying bright.
Out of reach. Out of sight.

Kris, My Childhood Friend

I never thought the day would come,
That I wouldn't see you.
But in the wind, he was calling,
And like the leaves, you fluttered away.
In Eden, you would be found.
A cherub filled flight, across the
Bleak night, utopian bound.
I remember the tempest that came,
And took my dear friend away.
Placed her in an early grave.
Never more, can I speak those words, never spoken.
You once brought us laughter, in the pouring rain.
Who now, will take away our pain?
I've looked at pictures.
They do you shame.
Only showing the outward frame.
I can cry my tears.
I can make my pleads,
But no one seems to answer me.
The friend I lost is there.
I can't seem to find the key,
That will bring her back to me.

The Road I Travel

You don't walk the road I travel.
You are happy when you feel alone and deserted.
You love the idea of love when love hurts.
You don't walk the road I travel,
When pain is what you seek.
I thought I could save you from depression; renew your belief in love.
But, you can't save someone who wants to dwell in darkness.
You are a man, who does not want the full cup of life,
Merely the bitter stench of spilled wine,
And the stains of a faded day gone by.
Go play your songs and live in the false melodies you spin.
Allow the world to look upon you with pity as a man, who walks alone,
On a path with no family, no home.
When I walk, the sun will be upon me.
The world will see a woman, who can hold her own,
A tale of courage, not one of sorrow but of a woman who faces the night as well as the day.
Go back now to your darkness, for I am a child of light.
Once my lover, now but a shadow, you don't walk the road I travel.

Samhain

"The Road" – McMillin '94

Angel not Far

My heart has cried. It has mourned.
My heart has pleaded to the Lord.
I long to see your moonlit face,
So warm, so alive, our last embrace.

I wake to find you gone from my grasp.
A memory is a warmth that cannot last.

From day to night, I watch the sky all along wondering why.
Why he took my love, my life, my very soul away?
I think of all the words I didn't say.

I look on a dove through eyes that weep.
Flying high above the pain I keep.
My love, my angel not far,
I promise to hold you in my heart once whole now scared.

My Darling, My Love

My darling, my love, I look on you from above.
I'm sorry. I had to leave,
But I will be in the dreams you weave.
It is hard to see you cry.
I know you don't understand all the reasons why.

My darling, my love, remember, all the things we've done.
How you were for me, the only one.
There are things now we cannot share,
But I will always be near.

My darling, my love, tuck in our child tight,
And I will be the blanket, which covers you at night.
I will comfort you from above,
With my everlasting love.

Only Friends

The one I love has betrayed thee,
Not once but twice.
T'is the ultimate slice.

To ask me to forget my wounds so deep.
To help him reach another.
To bring him to the one he dreams.
Only to know it is not me.

I am in a tunnel, where is the light
To guide me through the darkest of nights.

For him, I have committed a sin.
A sin to my heart's soul.
For him, I have made me the fool.

Angels Weep

In the morning Dad, I feel your love from the brilliant rays of sun.
In the dark, as I lay in bed, I remember all the things you've said.
No matter the trouble I would find, you would always understand.
Reaching out with a father's loving hand.
I wonder why God needed you now.
I know, I am not a child but there is so much more I wanted you to see.
Especially the man I could be, or seeing my first born smile.
They say you can see from heaven, but I still needed you for a little while …
My son, just beyond the golden gates, I see the weeping angels.
Weep not for me, but for you.
They feel your loss, and know your love for me is true.
But, I will brighten rainy days, and warm the coldest nights.
Even though for you I am out of sight.
And when you ask the question why, know that I am still alive.
My son, do not grieve, for I did not truly leave.
I have passed the gates of heaven, but I am not alone.
I am safe now, in my celestial home.
My soul is free of pain. If only you could see, what I have gained.
As I walk, in this cloudy mist, I think of all I will miss.
As I walk son, I think of you and all the things I hope you do.
I know there will always be a tear as long as you are there and I am here.

Once

Once I gave my heart to a boy not yet a man.
I got it back broken like the grain of sands.

Once I loved a man who was a boy.
I took his name but in return got a game.

Once I walked a path that made me the fool.
Now, I dare walk alone for the betterment of my soul.

Blind Heart

I rest my head on my pillow,
And ask the Gods why.
Why my heart could be so full,
Yet so empty inside?

Why did I trust?
I was blind in a storm of lies and lust.
She walked as a friend in the light,
But stalked in the cheating shadows of night.

She stole the one who was mine.
Together in lies they made my poor heart blind.

Seasons of Time ~ The Journey of Living

"Ice" ~ McMillin '96

Silent Lonely Tears

Too soft for others to hear,
Too great the pain for one to bear.
An unseen misery beneath,
Eyes, like windows, show the grief.
Not for others, for yourself you fool,
With happy fakeness that sickens the soul.
Now a shell, hiding tears within a well.
Bring me comfort under the pale moonlight,
These lonely tears help me sleep at night.
Cleansing the pain I cannot name,
Which enters the heart, but makes the mind insane.
No Hope.
No Love.
No Joy for me.
Looking for a future, which I cannot see.
Tears like rain fall across my face.
Hope, Love, Joy, lost to me.
Only tears across a window pane.
Shattered glass of a soul remains.

The One Who Gave Me Pain

Tears of panic ran down my face,
When I felt his cold embrace.
His dark, hard eyes are locked on mine.
In his gaze, I see the past.
The path I took with him, into a maze that never ends.
Blindly, I did walk, as he aimed a dagger, at my heart.
Now, here he is again.
My heart screams to run, but I remain.
Looking at the one I used to love, the one who gave me pain.
His eyes never change, as he reaches out for me.
I step without control, to his plead.
He holds me, like a fragile doll.
The winds of time blow down my wall. .
He whispers he cannot bear a day without me near.
Something tells me to get away, but I ignore the inner fear.
Love can lead you like a fool to hell.
Never hearing the warning, the voices yell.
For needing what I should not want can only lead to Misery.
In his other hand, yet another dagger I do not see.

Samhain

"Shattered" – McMillin '05

Why the Willow Weeps

Last night without you near, I had a dream a lover makes when there is more to bare. If I had a pen to paper it would have been the greatest thing I have written. The mind's thoughts and the heart's desires have converged into words yet more like visual emotions.

We sat under a willow in a purple mist for it is the willow that holds the unspoken feelings when lovers kiss. Though it was my dream, I weaved it not alone. I know that night your soul found mine and there our destinies intertwined.

I spoke to you words not from my lips and you heard my emotions not with your ears. It was the moment love is revealed like a magician with a trick, some could see it while for others it's missed.

You knew these words to be pure and from your heart you cried. Arms of oak you held me, lips like moss pressed soft against me and with your eyes I knew …
My love would be held by the willow and not you.

Arms of oak had let me go, and I must do the same. My soul touched yours this I will always know as thoughts of you I will let go. I woke to candle light and the sound of rain in the depth of night. My face wet from what could have been tears upon my pillow not shed by me but the willow …

Imbolc

"The rhythm of your heart fits the tune of my soul.
Now, love is dancing as time unfolds." ~ Kelly Ann

Love's New Birth

Loves new birth has come to me, on golden wings of time.
That flutter down, touch my heart, make me want to fly.
How, sudden it did come, without a sound.
No warning, for my once dying heart.
That once only pumped tears.
Now a flow of new life has sprung a flame.
That has turned my once gray heart red.
Never again will I feel the shame,
or death creeping my way.
For a new spirit runs through these veins.
This love, that was sent to me
From the back, of a golden dove.
Loves new birth has come to me, and has set my soul free.

Always in My Heart

As I sit, upon this chair.
I wonder, if you are near.
As I look, on to the sun.
I think of all the crazy things, you've done.
I remember, when you became an angel, in May.
Apart of my heart, I lost that day.
I remember, your style and grace.
The sparkle in you eyes, and the smile upon your face.
I remember, the good times, along with the bad.
How much more time, I wish we had.
I remember, all the stories you told,
But it is you. I want to hold.
As I hear, the breeze blow by.
In this peaceful moment, I will cry.
As I free my mind, It is you I will find.
As I think of you, in the heavens above,
I know you're looking out, for the ones you love.
Never will we part,
For you will always be in my heart...

In Loving Memory of Mary Salopek Lynch
- May 28, 1997 -

Imbolc

"Above" – McMillin '05

Mother

In the morning, I feel your love,
From the brilliant rays of sun.
In the dark, as I lay in bed.
I remember all the things you've said.
With all that I have done.
You would always understand.
Reaching out with a mother's loving hand.
I wonder why my God needed you now.
I know am not a child.
But, there is so much I wanted you to see.
Especially the young man, I could be.
I wanted you at my wedding,
And to see my first born smile.
I know you can see from heaven,
But I still wanted you here for a little while.
Now as I close my eyes,
I know we said our last good bye.

A Mother's Song

I will always be there.
I will always love you.
I will wipe away your tears.
All the things I say and do,
You may not understand,
But, they were done, with
A mother's loving hand.

At night, when you are scared,
I will always be there.
I will protect you when I can.
I will take away your fears,
With this loving hand.

Some day when you have babies
Of your own. You will know and
Understand this loving hand.

Far from now, when I must leave,
Near you I will always be.
Guiding you when I can,
With a mother's loving hand.

Sleep Tight

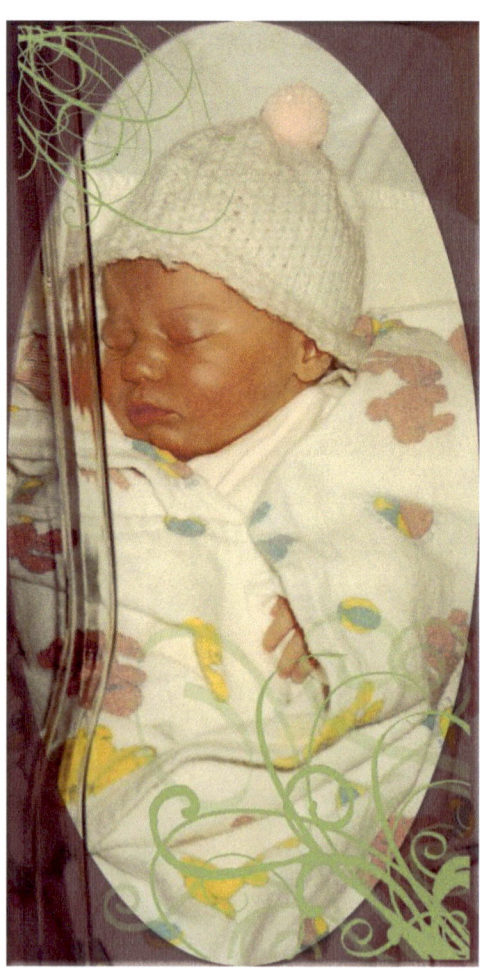

Sleep tight my child,
All through the night.

Don't let your pain, gain one
Ounce, of your dreams so bright.

Hold back your tears,
And let go of your fears.

As you fade away, into a misty new day.
Only let love touch your heart,
And your dreams will not fall apart.

So sleep tight my love,
And let the angels dance above.

Singing music, in the light.
Bringing peaceful dreams, in the night.

Mother's Day

To a child, there is only one.
A mother watches them from day one.
A mother shows them love.
Even when the bad deeds have been done.
They bring out the strength,
And courage in the little ones.
Who someday will face the cold world.
While always knowing, they are loved.

First Star

As I sit, on my soft seat out in the open air.
I look up and see the first star appear.
I go here to let my spirits flow and breath.
The sun has fallen from the sky, like a kite.
That was flying high. Now, I sit and wait
Anticipating the moon of silvery gray.

As I gaze, into the sky. I realize. I am but a
Minute piece of life. Yet, a piece that must
Be there. For the puzzle looks barren, if just
One piece is not there.

As I listen, to the wispy air. I can hear the creatures,
Of the night. The footsteps of those that are small.
The soft hum of tiny wings. I can smell the light
Scent of pine, and I feel more at home here, then
In my wooden home.

As I wonder, if romance has left our world.
Replaced by a bitterness. If more people would step
Outside their wooden homes, and gaze up
At the sky. Would they see, that they are but a piece?
A piece of something greater than the eye can see,
Or the brain can imagine.

But, the sky fills more of stars, and the first star
Is growing harder to find. I try to let the scenery
Set in, and I am reminded that life travels fast.
If one does not take the time to notice.
He might not get the chance to understand.

Into the Mystic

When we kiss.
We' re into the mystic bliss.
Nobodies the same,
In this place without blame.
For it knows no shame.

In here we just start,
The eternal heart a flame,
With hope, dreams and love.
We are two people, but as one.

Who shall never part,
Without a piece, of the others eternal heart.
For our love lit the flame,
That will always stay.

Always burning for the other.
Never looking for another.
Always wanting each other.

Into the mystic part,
Of the others eternal heart.

Imbolc

"Mystic" – McMillin '05

Time is All We Need

At first, we were two stars.
Who collided, in the heavens.
The light from us, shined so bright.
It could pierce, the darkest night.

But the waters of despair,
Would cause a fog to appear.
We would lose our path that day,
Across the Milky Way.
It seemed like never,
Would our paths come together.

But time is all we need,
For our two paths to meet.
Now two stars sit.
Where a fire was lit.
In this light above,
Forever in a constellation of love…

My Love

Hold me in your arms, before you leave.
Keep love, in our heart, where it should be.
Kiss me once before you go,
And know that our love will grow.
Whisper softly that you need me,
And I will do the same.
Your touch gives me strength, to watch you walk away.
Go quickly my love, so you won't see.
The tears I'll cry. When you must leave.
Your love will hold me tight.
While I lay awake.
I'll be wishing you were here tonight.

Friends

They are the ones that share.
The ones that care.
The ones who mend a broken heart.
They give you courage. When life seems dark.
They can show your beauty, from within.
When you stumble. They help lift your chin.
Without their smiling face, it would truly be, a lonely place.

Seasons of Time ~ The Journey of Living

Sun

Misty rain,
Pouring and shinning,
The gold is as close as the imagination.
Rainbow

Birds

Loving creatures,
Sings and sources,
Harmless, peaceful, loving
Creatures untouched by,
Life's inhumanity.

Doves

Brothers

Brothers are not perfect.
They pick, tease and fight.
They can make you erupt, like a volcano
full of might.
But, brothers will also lend a hand,
That will guide you through the night.
These are the tender times,
That are weaved through out our life.
A single thread, a special bond,
We sew between our souls.

Friendship

Is two baby cubs.
Who tumble, jump, bite and fight,
In the dark damp cave.
Passing, the long boring days away.

I Say I Love You

At times when I am happy,
At times when I am sad,
My heart even speaks it softly,
At times you've made me mad.

What do they mean those four letters in a row?
When I speak them, do you know?

For me when they are spoken,
It's a symbol of my heart's token.

It means your soul comforts me like
The steady sound of rain.

It means your body shelters me,
From the world's harshness and pain.

It means the touch of your hands awaken,
The fire of my skin's senses.

It means without you there'd be darkness,
Where joy could never win.

L-O-V-E is the translation of my soul,
Where the mysteries of my heart unfold.

It is a way for me to express your worth,
When life changes you are my true north…

What I am Thinking Of

Feeling as if my body rests upon a cloud, soft, warm endless.
A touch that sends a so seductively addictive to my core.
Sensation of warm tender lips upon my skin.
A conversational depth that invites the mind to expand, absorb live.
What I am thinking of is you.

The Sunshine of My Life

A rose at dawn,
A cuddly puppy,
A sunrise,
But most of all you.
The way you walk.
The way you talk.
I watch your every move.
The words you say, linger in the air.
I can feel your warmth so near.
You are the special one.
The one I hold so dear,
In my heart and soul.
Just the way you look,
So perfect and pure.
I'll never let you go, without a fight.
You are the sunshine of my life.

Finding My Way to You

Until dreams reach the light,
I will think of you tonight.

My knight in shining armor came true,
The very day I met you.

Within the crowd and smoke, a hat of golden yellow,
Would lead my eyes to this fellow.

Across the room I knew,
There was something I had to say to you.

Lost in your smile, I would linger for a little while.

A chance I would take,
As a conversation I started about the race.

To my delight, we would talk into the night.

But here our story will not end,
For I have married my best friend.

When It's True

When it's true love.
Not much in this world, can make you blue.
The little things I've done before.
All seems to be new.

When cradled like a babe.
I feel safe from harms way.
In the whispers, of the night,
There is a warmth, that holds me tight.

There is a fire, that burns deep inside.
Only one can make this flame.
My heart only thinks of you,
And I shall never be the same.

When it's true love, it will never go away.
You've held me tight, from the coldness, of the night.
You've cradled me in your arms,
And kept me safe, from any harm.

Serenity by the Lake

In a time when I did not feel special,
You helped to see I was.

In a time when the ground beneath me would shake,
You offered a steady hand to take.

In a time when my world was full of strangers,
You showed me there were friends.

In a time when life went dark,
Your smile brought in the light.

In a time when I could have lost faith,
Your arms renewed my strength.

In a time when I could not sleep,
Your comfort came in a heartbeat.

In the calming of a sunrise,
I sit back, relax and close my eyes.

Slowly images play of our first date;
Talking, dinner and serenity by the lake.

Imbolc

"Lover's Lake" – McMillin '11

When Love Shines on Me

Oh, how happy I would be. If love
Would shine on me.
Having you hold me tight.
Knowing these feelings were right.

There is so much we could be,
If love shines on me.
I would bare any pain,
To know you feel the same.

When we're together.
I want to know. It is forever.
When we're apart.
I want your love, to fill my heart.

I know this could be true.
Every time I get close to you.
I know what I want to be,
Just you with me.

The Beginning

Do you remember when are hands first met and a new relationship's first test?

Remember when, we first kissed?
Could we have seen that was the start, of something between you and me?

Remember the heat we would find, when our bodies first entwined?

Remember how our bodies swayed
As we began to dance, on our wedding day?

Remember our youthful days
Where the love and passion would never fade?

I remember all of this,
When I touch your tender lips.

"Life" ~ McMillin '05

Bealtaine

"Time has no meaning. Distance just a number, when the spirit takes flight to a harbor in the night." ~ Kelly Ann

Time's Whisper

In the Summer Breeze, wild flowers brush against my knees as
The sun Dances upon my skin. A new era begins…

Like the fist whispers of my youth, which now shelter me as a roof. In the milky white clouds
where only dreams are allowed there within time's whisper abound.

The Road

There are many roads to life,
And it may take awhile, to find the one that's right.
Some may lead to fame.
While others lead to shame,
But none will ever stay the same.
Some you travel from fear,
But ultimately they take you nowhere.
No matter which way you will go.
There is something that will always be.
There is a road out there, for you and me.
It's your dreams you may find,
On these endless roads of time.

Angel of the Night

Angel of the night help me understand.
Hold this weeping heart steady with your loving hand.

Scotty was given to the world this July day.
Then the winds of October would carry him away.

Angel of the night can it be,
That the years without him are almost three.

Angel of the night with your face unknown.
Embrace me with your gentle wings so I shall not stand along.

My angel, there is one thing I need.
I ask of you what I cannot do.
Give my baby brother a birthday kiss from me.

Bealtaine

"The Water's Rush" – McMillin '04

Sweet Child of Mine

There was a day.
No not far from May.
When I discovered.
I would be a mother.

How I felt such joy.
Did not matter, whether girl or boy.
But, I was scared.
I had so many fears.
I knew it would not be long,
That you would be here.
There was so much to prepare.

So much happened along the way.
My grandma was gone, in the month of May.
There would be an uncle. You'd never know.
He was my brother.
He died, before I became a mother.
But, it was you who made me strong.
When my life seemed wrong.

It was the 24th of December.
A day, I shall always remember.

For it was that day.
God had brought you, to me.
A mother, I will for always be.

Now, as I look into your eyes. I see
All the wonderful things you could be.
As I touch your tiny hand,
So much more to life I understand.

Photo by Mary Ann McMillin

Reality's Dream

When day gives way and fades to dark.
I reflect on passion found in a tranquil park,
Of arms reaching out to hold the other tight.
May these memories of exquisite moments
Guide me through the night.

Somewhere between words spoken
And the body's sweet motion.
The heart of a woman found
The soul of a man.

Fate set a course, neither had planned.
Somehow in reality and a dream,
Where hope once forgotten now gleams.

The heart and the soul are no longer alone.
Walking destiny together may they
Find their way home.

On the path to finding answers
Through pain and love revealed.
These two tattered spirits may learn to heal.

Riding the wings of time that flutter.
Minutes to days on a journey to the other.

Now, dark gives way to day's first light.
Walking between reality and memory's sight.
The hours spent together may seem so few,
But cherished are these moments with you…

More Than a Thought to Me

As I sit here waiting to get through yet another day,
My thoughts drift to California in the sweetest of ways.
I think of the smile that lights up my face.
Just a thought is all it takes … just words from your lips with no one to embrace.
These two bodies that cannot entwine yet connect deeper than any soul could find.
Not minutes or days or even weeks can explain – why I feel this to be true.
There is just something about the talks with you.
A comfort of home within each word,
A feeling of worth – a value I should say.
I am too a person … with freedoms like a bird in motion.
A longing so deep during times we cannot speak,
Almost a pain or a fire of the purest desire, my body shakes as if a live-wire.
Intensity of the flames beyond my reach,
Yet like feet to a path I am moved towards the heat of the western sun.
My nature to shelter and hide has been erased,
As I only want to open my gates – like a petal from a bud.
I am washing away the pain of the past like the filth of mud.
A new hope's seed planted where the soul would hide.
In a dream perhaps for I can't believe my eyes.
A heart with scars – dark and cold.
Now beats and feeds the soul.

Bealtaine

"California Dreams" – McMillin '09

Love's Prayer

Dear God,

There is a man, and with him, I will always stand. No other man can pull apart the golden band he placed upon my heart. To you I pray, for a while, with me he'll stay.

Through storms great and mild, he has been there for me and my child. He has a soul like no other I've found.

Skin like thread, we're woven tight. I sleep with him, throughout the night. During any troubles, that life may bring. It is to him that I cling.

With this man, I want to be. For in his eyes, my future I can see. Our path in life I pray, you will light and guide the way.

So to you God, I pray, for a while, with him I'll stay. Until the day we must part, I pray in heaven you reunite these two hearts.

Summer's Long Hot Nights

Summer's long hot nights,
Where everything feels right,
And the moon is bright.

A hot breeze, washes over your face.
Giving off, a loving embrace.
The kind that makes your heart beat race.

The summer nights make you strong.
Even when things go wrong.

Just look all around.
You're bound to see, the colors
Of the night sky. The milky white light,
Of the moon up high,
And the golden stars afar.
The pitch black blanket, falling upon it all.
These are summer's long hot nights...

Seasons of Time ~ The Journey of Living

"Water's Edge" ~ McMillin '94

I Don't Want to Wait

During the sunrise, of early morning.
When the grass, glistens with dew.
Bringing the first light, of dawn,
Making our spirits renew.

While walking in the woods,
With the first leaves of Fall.
Dancing, in the air, like a cool wispy wall.

A cool breeze blowing by.
Where the lake's water reaches land.
Sitting on grass made of sand.

Lying on a blanket, in a field.
Looking upon the sky, no longer blue.
Watching the light, of the stars, shine true.

These are the places. I might find,
For our bodies to entwined.
But, I don't want to wait,
To open up my heart's gate.
These words I want to say.
I love you on this day.

Heat

I lay here, in this empty bed.
While thoughts of you run
Through my head.
With every breath I take.
I think of the love, we will make.
The way our bodies swayed, with flesh
Against each other tight.
Creating a heat that still keeps me warm tonight.
This desire of you I fear will burn,
Until every part of you, I've learned.
A lust that makes me strong,
In what way could this be wrong?
Until we no longer part at the break of day,
In my soul's fire, you will stay.

Inside the Heart

I know there is something I feel,
but I have to wonder if it's real.
Can't you see? My heart is pleading.
It's silently bleeding.
It needs to know.
Some how will you show?
Where all these feelings will go.
You know how I've been burned.
From false promises, I have learned.
It's not the words. I want to hear.
Just please, show me you'll be there.
With everything you do.
Let me know. What I feel is true.
Let me see that there will be,
a place inside your heart, for me.

Seasons of Time ~ The Journey of Living

"A Dream" ~ McMillin '08

A Lover's Dream

Last night I had a dream that I wanted to tell you how much you mean to me and the love I feel for you. I started to compose the words in my mind and instantly I knew this would be the greatest thing I have ever written so I grabbed a book to catch every word. Even I knew words like these come but once in a lifetime.

Then under a weeping willow I read the words to you and you cried for it was pure love -- the kind that is spoken only to a few but desired by all.

Then amongst the deepest kiss I awoke to find it just a dream. I tried to scrap the depth of my mind for a single word I had spoken to you; even the title was a blank.

Though I was sadden to find these words not in light remembered I knew in that moment that they were heard for that was not merely a dream. But my soul speaking to yours and I know you heard me for the warmth of that dream only comes from love. I believe my mind can't recall for the words were so pure that we awake would never know the beauty that our souls could hear in the night of a lover's dream.

Three Words

Day by day. Piece by piece.
Being near you eats away, this wall I keep.
Week by week. Kiss by kiss.
When alone, it's your warmth. I miss. I know there will come a day.
When this wall. I bare will fade, and these three words I'll be free to say.
Until then, may you hear these silent words,
From my heart, and know there is a special place in there for you.
When we're apart. May you hear those words,
In the way I kiss. In everything I do. May you hear the words,
And when I say them, you will know it's true.

Tender Nights

Darkness like fingers weave throughout the sky.
Eyes look upon me where hands are sky.

Arms reaching out to hold me tight,
In moments spent together in the night.

When I open the petal of my soul,
Ecstasy comes within the heart's pull.

Your touch like branded flesh stays with me.
The stain of your lips on mine,
Your scent lingers like burning wood and sweet wine.

Drawn to your nectar, like a sickness to a cure.
Flesh pressed to flesh, as if within me, you haven't left.

To each whim the body bends, until we find the journey's end.
In the dawn fears may renew, but tender are these nights with you.

The Man I Love

Lying next, to the man, that lies next to me.
I think about all we can be.
Both faced with life's uncertainties.
In the night, when I watch him sleep,
Sometimes I softly weep.
Trying to hide my fears,
While emotions run so deep.
I wonder if he knows,
For I cannot speak.
With tender whispers and a kiss.
I try to let him know,
How much I love him so.
I lay my hand, upon his chest.
It rises and falls, with every breath.
With every breath, my love grows strong.
How can my feelings be wrong?
Draped in his arms, like a blanket of warmth.
My soul no longer hurts.
This man I love, with all my heart.
With this man, love feels new.
There is nothing, I would not do.
Lying next to the man that lies next to me.
I close my eyes, and hope
This will always be...

Bealtaine

"Calm" – McMillin '94

If you Ask Me...

All my truths could be revealed to you,
My pain, my passion within these eyes of blue.
If you ask me…

The chemistry of the heart can be fleeting,
Leaving you shattered and bleeding.
Then bare your soul for me to stay,
And I will mend and guide your heart along the way.
If you ask me…

In my world, where evil takes all things safe.
In your arms like an altar, I could find my faith.
If you ask me…

As a glove to your body I will mold,
At the depth of darkness, I will be the light you hold.
If you ask me…

In my life where words were broken,
I could trust in promises from your lips spoken.
If you ask me…

Release the yearning to dancing desires of the flesh,
Can be two souls greatest quest.

The caress of my hands gently soothing, enticing sparks to flames,
Removing the walls allowing only passion to remain.
If you ask me…

I can be the water that quenches thirst,
A tender touch that heals your hurt.
If you ask me…

Within you, I have come to live.
To you all of me I would give.
If you ask me…

In finding you – I found me,
But what of us will come to be…

Others will live, never to have felt what I now know.
You are a rare gem, found among the many stones.
I will hold you to me dearly or I will let go.
If you ask me…

Search your heart, question your soul,
Find your truth like keys to unlock life's hold.
Allow the dreams of your heart to unfold.
Allow the happiness of your soul to be told.
Is all I ask of you…

In the Whisper of a Wave

The water of my soul renewed,
By these tender moments spent with you.

Do not be fooled, by words I do not speak.
Emotions like a currant run deep.
I long to be the water in which you play.
One only needs to listen to the whisper of a wave…

When you need arms to surround you – I offer mine.
May the harbor of my body be a haven, but not the suffocating kind.
You are safe within my shores,
For weepy eyes see like a dolphin, you need more.
You are bound for the solitary freedom of the deep.
You find life, in the adventures you seek.

Restless with the ticking clock.
Ice once thick upon the rocks.
Now, in the spring gives way.
Shorter grows your time to splash and play.

Why do I then reach for depths, I have not known.
Is it your energy or the pleasure of your tone?
I thought the giver in me long ago died,
But you the moon pull at my tides.

So, I am in your world, in glimpses you can see.
Yet, ever trying hard not to hold you too close to me.
I offer comforts of the night.
Until the morning, you take flight.

Bringing reprieve as we part,
Memories of this dance wash over the heart.
As a tongue licks its wound, I will mend.
But, until you leave my dear friend.

Will lay me down before you like the sand upon the beach.
At the water's rush where earth and water meet,
Not fearing the erosion of our walls, we must be brave,
To hear the treasure in the whisper of a wave....

"Whimsical" ~ McMillin '05

About the Author

About the Author

Kelly Ann McMillin was born in 1975 to Larry and Mary Ann McMillin and raised in Western Pennsylvania with her two brothers, Bryan and Scott. Her love of poetry developed at a young age along with her other artistic skills. She graduated Slippery Rock High School in 1994 with her brother Scott and the Butler County Vocational Technical School Graphic Arts program.

In 1999, Kelly Ann was diagnosed with left-side ulcerative colitis, an inflammatory bowel disease. She feels many others suffer with digestive disorders but they are reluctant to seek treatment or to even discuss with others their personal experiences. She hopes that by being forward about her condition that others will not feel as isolated and be encouraged to continue to pursue their dreams. Kelly Ann donates her time to the Crohn's and Colitis Foundation of America and she started the team "Sugar Shack" with her daughters and participates in the "Take Steps to Be Heard for Crohn's and Colitis" fundraising walk. Learn more about Crohn's and Colitis Foundation of America at www.CCFA.org .

Kelly Ann graduated Cum Laude in 2008 at Point Park University with a Bachelor of Science in Business focusing on marketing and public relations. While continuing her education, Kelly Ann worked as a Community Coordinator for Trib Total Media, Pittsburgh newspaper group. She managed over eight online community sites for the Pittsburgh Trib and Gateway Newspapers. In 2007, she joined Black Box Network Services, independent provider of communications and infrastructure solutions, as Marketing Coordinator with primary role to develop, launch and manage Black Box's social media marketing plans. In April of 2009, Kelly Ann became a member of Cambridge Who's Who of Executives, Professional and Entrepreneurs.

In 2010, Kelly Ann joined the National Association of Professional Women (NAPW) and took on the role of Director of Social Media and mentor for the NAPW Pittsburgh Chapter. In late 2011, she would become Chapter President and will complete her term in December of 2013. She is also an active member of the Slippery Rock University Communication Dept. Advisory Board, and supports the Army of Women and the Wild Dolphin Foundation. She believes real change will only occur when the individual makes an effort towards bettering the lives of others.

Kelly Ann married Keith V. Wagner and she enjoys spending time with her two daughters, Samantha and Karaline, and their dogs Boomer, Gizzy and Brandy. She currently resides in Western Pennsylvania with her family and continues to express her emotions through art.

Her next endeavor is to establish the Tri-Women Society, a women's group that focuses on creativity, feminine strength and hearth, which are the three aspects to the triple Goddess Brighid. Learn more about her organization at www.triwomensociety.com .